sage¹ (s j)

One venerated for experience, judgment, and wisdom.

adj. sag·er, sag·est

1. Having or exhibiting wisdom and calm judgment.

    2. Proceeding from or marked by wisdom and calm judgment: *sage advice.*

3. *Archaic* Serious; solemn.

Sage - a mentor in spiritual and philosophical topics who is renowned for profound wisdom
Hakham - a Hebrew title of respect for a wise and highly educated man mahatma - (Hinduism) term of respect for a brahmin
sage mentor, wise man - a wise and trusted guide and advisor

Pen and Paper

Pen and Paper
My two friends

When we meet
Our stories never end...

One sits in front of me
The other holds my hand

Now we are together
Let Poetry begins...

Pen and Paper
My two friends

We show the world
The stories within

He spoke, I listened
We write again

My life, Our journeys
these words, now Begin

This is Our story, three friends
The End...

From Living to being Risen...

Release to Grow

There are only three things you need to let go of:

Judging, Controlling, and Being Right.

There times when we can not change who we are and

Times when we try to make people what we think we want them to be.

Release these three and enjoy life as it is and people as they are.

Plant a Seed and Watch it Grow....

Planting a Seed and Watching them Grow...

Plant a Seed and Watch it Grow
The years are few
How fast they go.

Months grow short,
The days close fast
Time is quick, now it's the past

We need to plant a seed
And watch it grow
The young we must show

The nights are gone
The days are old
These times we lived
Are all no more

We have to plant the seed
And hope it grows
The young ones we were but now we're old

We need to spread the knowledge
To the young before their time
To walk in peace
Or we are, no more..

Plant a Seed and Watch it Grow

You Don't hear me
but are you Listening

When we listen,

trying to understand each other

Not listening, just to reply....

Now, we can begin to communicate

 in relationships...

This will give us the opportunity to speak freely

Then we can begin to understand

each other

in a new way...

Just saying

Plant a Seed and Watch it Grow...

I am Stronger than you

Be humble and strong as you endure the pains of life

Let no man's word make you feel small

Remember the one that speaks these words

Are smaller then you...

Just saying

Plant a Seed and Watch it Grow

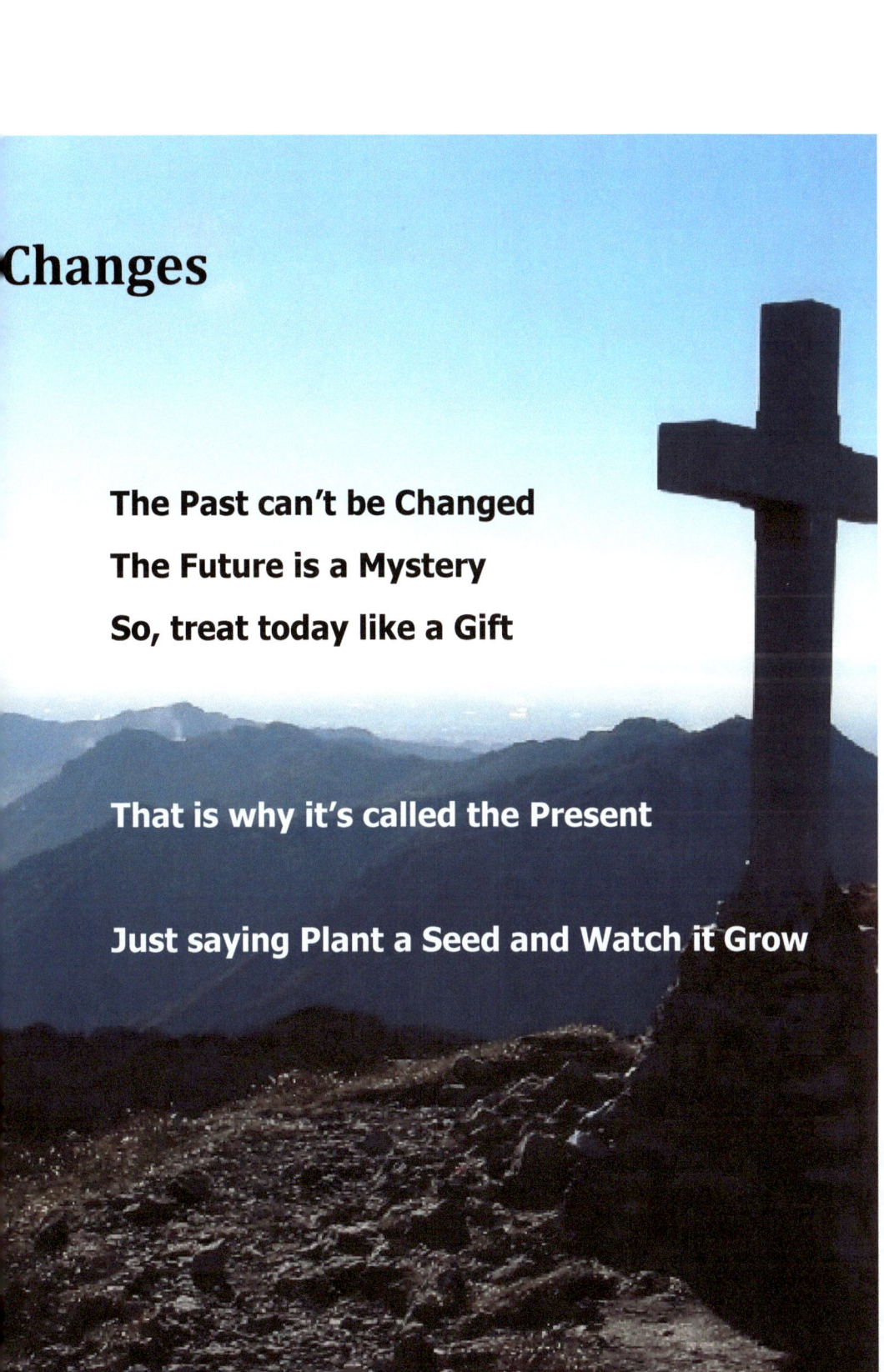

Changes

The Past can't be Changed

The Future is a Mystery

So, treat today like a Gift

That is why it's called the Present

Just saying Plant a Seed and Watch it Grow

My Good Friend

As I sit here all alone
No one to talk to
No one to phone

Where is that friend
Someone close to me
Where is my friend when I'm in need

So I sit all alone
with pen and paper
Holding what's unknown

I wait for an answer
I wait til the end
Another day and still no friend

So I say to myself
As I hold back what's within
Then I say a little prayer...

It is me God
And he says
I'm always listening

'My Good Friend'

Darkness to Light

As we walk down the road of life there will always be forks in the road

One side darkness and the other side light

No one wants to travel in the darkness

We have to understand the darkness we have inside

So look inside through the darkness for your light and let it shine

One must understand Ones self

And the darkness before knowing who you are in the light

Then and only then can one help and do right for others.

The Girl of my Dreams...

The Girl of my Dreams

Is my Girl no Mo

I open my heart

Now I close the door

She smile and laugh

But was never true

The Girl of my Dreams

Time told me it was not you

I wanted her to be the girl for me

But the girl of my dreams will never be

The Girl of my Dreams

Is my Girl no More

I will never call you

A bitch not even a Hoe

You could have had everything

But Girl no damn Mo

The Girl of my Dreams

Is My Girl No More

Believe

Don't be blind to the truth that is in front of you...

Don't be deaf to the voice inside of you

Don't be hurt when it wasn't love from the start

Don't believe when you know it's not true

And remember to just believe in you

Just saying Plant a Seed and Watch it Grow

My Soulmate

You're my Soulmate, but I don't know why
is it your touch, your smile or the sparkle in your eyes

I write to you, telling you the truth
not just silly words that sound so cute

I'm not sure what to say or what to do
Because I'm slowly falling in love with you
To hold your hand, to feel your touch
so many little things that make me love you so much

Your lips meet my lips, our very first kiss
it felt so right how could I resist

The way that you kiss me, fills me with desire
to hold you, Would be like warmth of a fire

The dreams that I dream, they are all about you
the possibilities I see, the things that we can do

But to finish this puzzle that lies in my heart
from deep in my soul, you are a very important part

The whisper of your voice, the warmth of your touch
the words may vary, but never can be said too much

I love you

Hearts Broken

Love is found deep in our Hearts

But words were spoken

A Heart was broken

Tears fell fast

So this love did not last

To forgive and forget

Is not so easy to do

Now, I will move on without you

But first I'm letting know

These words are short

Memories not sweet

Time apart is what I seek

God Forgives ALL

So I trust in Him

But you on the other hand

Hmmm

thee
END

the Problem

**You can not solve a problem
thinking the same way
that created the problem...**

**Just saying
Plant a seed and watch it grow...
Be Bless and walk in Peace today**

A Wrong way, to Love ?

There is no wrong way to love, somebody

If you truly love that somebody…

And it is wrong to say you love, somebody

If that somebody is someone you don't

love…

But there is a wrong way to tell somebody

That you don't love that someone

anymore…

But remember one thing,

You can't love

anybody…

Until you can love yourself

Because you must be that somebody…

First…

How Do I Know Who Lies ???

How Do I Know Who Lies ???

Do you see it in their smile or the look in their eyes

Do they speak the truth or only lies?

How Do I Know Who Lies ???

They say "I love you" But tell it to everyone too

Why do they say it if their words are not true?

How Do I Know Who Lies ???

A Man A Woman and A Friend

Who will tell the truth in the end

How Do I Know Who Lies ???

I listen and believed

But never knew it would be you...

How Do I Know Who Lies ???

My God, I know you will pull me through

Because, Only you told me the truth....

A New Start

The End of the Year fades out

A New Year comes in and it screams and shouts

One year of Heartaches, Lost Love Ones

Jobs gone and Little Ones Mov'n on...

A Choice was made, A Heart must Break

Did you learn from love you lost, those words not spoken

Learning, Understanding and Sharing

Are such Simple things to do...

Well we Think too Much,

Lov'n too Little...

Like Sinning while trying to be True

Is this Me, Is this You,

This is the World

And Another Year

To Start Anew ...

the Spark that makes me smile

I loved you before, you know what love was

I will loved you until ,you know what love can be...

I love you now , you know what love is

I'm your dad and I love you

From the day you were born to day I die

You are the light of my life

The apple of my eye,

you are the spark that makes me smile

the beat of my heart, the pain in my butt

I wouldn't change a thang no matter what....

Love you baby girl...

Your Daddy,

Loving You

Looking into your eyes
I don't know what to say
It was as if God
Molded you from clay
Your lips are soft and sweet
Your smile a beautiful treat
Every time we meet
You take my breath away
Searching for the right words
To make you stay
So look into my eyes
And see me through my heart
You were the one for me
From the very start
If I had only one wish
And wishes came true
That wish would be
Me Loving You...

Imagine

I imagine you and I, walking alone in the woods
The first rays of the morning sunshine are flowing
Through the trees on us and warming our bodies as
We walk along the trail.

As we walked and talked we found a nice grassy clearing.
We sat and shared our thoughts while holding hands.
Your warm soft hands in mine. Then I tuned to look into
Your eyes. Your eyes smile at mine and our lips softly meet.
begin to get passionate. We embraced out bodies pressing together.
We lied down on the soft grass, You laid on top of me. I held you tight to me
With loving you on my mind. Our hearts beating faster as we remove are clothes.
No one will see this moment of love, but the flowers and the trees.

You're a fine lover who is striving to make me happy in every possible way. At that
Moment we are about to explode. I take you in my arms and kiss you.
I kiss you deeper and harder

We climax together and our bodies tremble. You smile and glow with love. We remain in each
others arms until the passion we've shared has surpassed all other thoughts. And
We will always remain in each other mind and hearts.

**Can you imagine that
This could become true
I can
How about
You...**

Imagine

One's action can inspire others

The wise look ahead to see what is coming,
but fools deceive themselves in to what the believe they want to see.

Fools don't see beauty in everyday things, they only see negative...
Always have something to say, I wish things were better,
I wish I had this or that...

Never hear them say, I did my best and I'm getting better.
I don't need that because I have this.
I love you for who you are and we will make it better together...

Leaving Memoirs

To my Family and Friends
Remember the these words I'm telling you
Don't just spend time with your
 Children Family or Friends
Leave Memoirs with Them

Good and Bad
Right and Wrong
They will remember

The question is
What Memoirs will
You leave them??
DREAMS I hope

Plant a Seed and Watch it Grow

My Friends and Family

Give **Thanks**...

Share your life and beliefs with each other

Leave a memory with someone you

Love...

Teach someone from what you have learned

Listen to a friend in need

Forgive...

Give your Soul to God

Live with Love

Understand without Judging

Now the question is:

Not , what can you **Do**

but

What **will** you **Do**?

Complete

Finish each day and be done with it.

Tomorrow is a new day, start fresh and complete what you can...

Don't worry so much about the little things, complete the task at hand...

Issues can be fixed, but problems can't

So don't make yesterday's **Issue**

Today's **problem**...

Just saying Plant a Seed and Watch it Grow

Yesterday

A Mother dies
A Son's last goodbye
Now my brother's gone
Because of **Yesterday**

Sitting here alone
My daughter is grown
With a family of her very own
Because of **Yesterday**

I was meek and weak
But now I speak
Of the pain inside
Because of **Yesterday**

Teaching words of the Sage
While reflecting the seeds I've sown
I planted them now their grown
  Because of **Yesterday**

So live for today
  Grow for Tomorrow
    Because you can't Change

        Yesterday

MY BROTHER

My Brother,
Her Lover,
Their Father,
His Son,
Your Friend
Like no other…

A Helping Hand, A Shoulder to Lean On…
Someone Who Will Beat Your Butt,
But Protect you No Matter What,

He's My Brother

Ups and Downs
Cry'n and Smile'n
Ly'n and Doing Wrong
We Stood Together, Cause we could

He's My Brother

Her Lover,
There Father,
His Son,
Your Friend
Like no other…

He's Mine
And Yours….

Thank you Lord for
MY BROTHER….

You can't take it with you

For sure there a few things on Earth you can't take with you

Your **Heart**, Your **Body** and Your **Mind**

But you can leave behind

Your **Love**, Your **Essence** and Your **Memories**

So share your life with someone

So you can live forever in their heart,

their mind and their life…

Just saying

Plant a seed and watch it grow

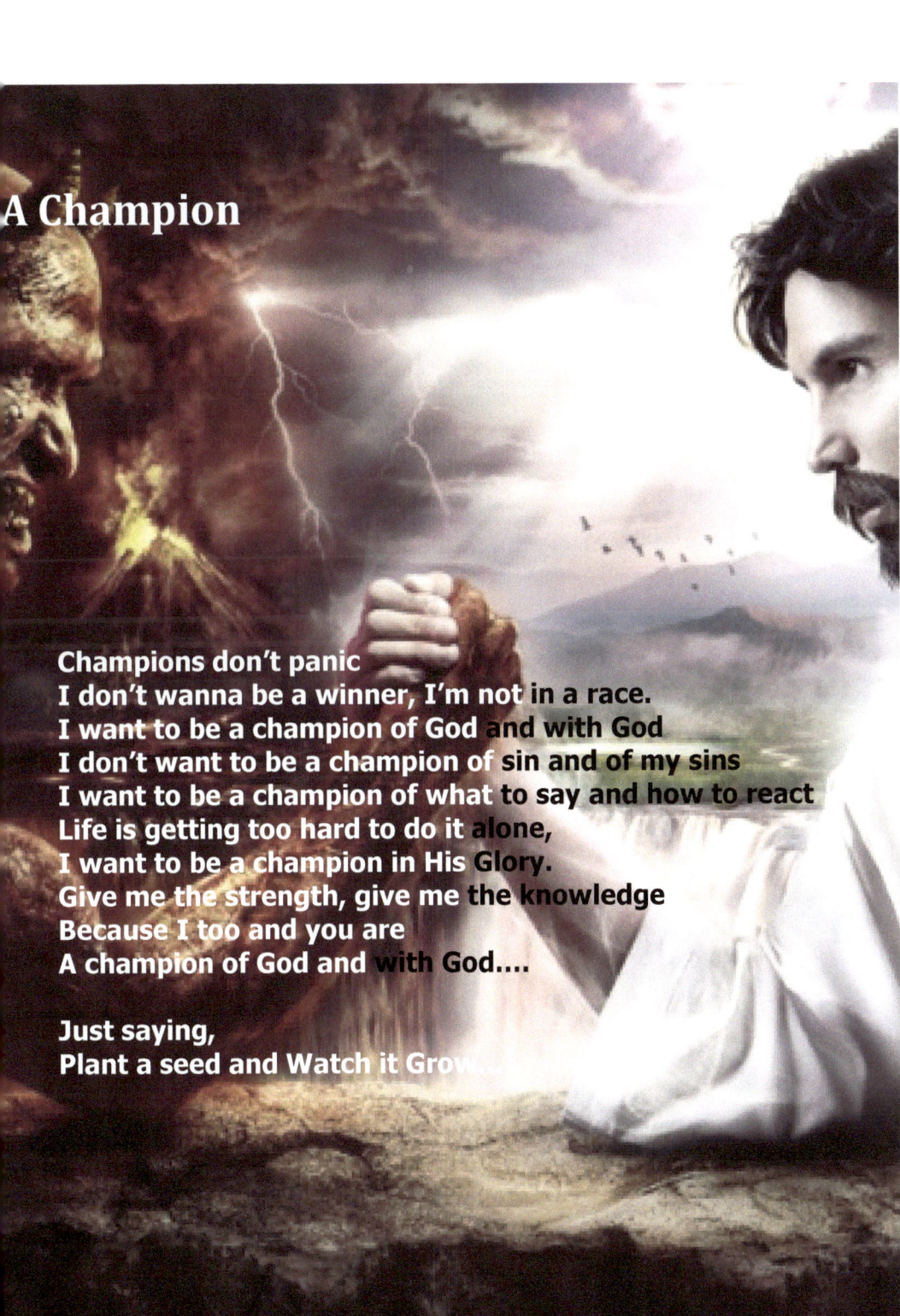

A Champion

Champions don't panic
I don't wanna be a winner, I'm not in a race.
I want to be a champion of God and with God
I don't want to be a champion of sin and of my sins
I want to be a champion of what to say and how to react
Life is getting too hard to do it alone,
I want to be a champion in His Glory.
Give me the strength, give me the knowledge
Because I too and you are
A champion of God and with God….

Just saying,
Plant a seed and Watch it Grow.

Everyone has Something to Say

Some don't know ,how to say it

Some don't want ,to hear it

Some think they ,know it

Some just don't ,know shit

But if you hear it in your heart

Don't let anyone stop you from,

Just saying it

I felt It

Then wrote it

Now, you read it

So together we can spread it…

Just saying it,

Plant a Seed and Watch it Grow…

To do right

The *Desire* to do **right** sometimes,

Over shadows the *Purpose* of doing **right**

Then our will overlooks the will of others

Now **Respect** for them is lost.

So, be *kind* in your **words**

And be kind to others

The only thing we can control

Is how we react to each other.

BE TRUE....

never say I love you, if you don't

never say I'll be there, if you wont

don't hit me and say ' it hurts me more then it hurts you'

Why is it that I make you happy and you make me so sad

Why do you turn things around and make me bad.

I told you to be true to me and I'll be true to you

But now I see ...

the only thing I need to learn is that

       'I don't need you....'

Changes

The Past can't be Changed

The Future is a Mystery

So, Treat today like a Gift

That is why It's called the Present

Just Saying

Plant a Seed and Watch it Grow

Relationships

You can **love** someone, be **in love** with someone or (just) **be in like**.

Never get them mixed up in a relationship...

We have to consider just because you are **in love** or **love** or **in like**

that doesn't mean the other person feels the same way.

What we need to do in relationships is understand don't just compromise

By understanding we can have balance but remember communication is everything

Just saying

Plant a Seed and Watch it Grow

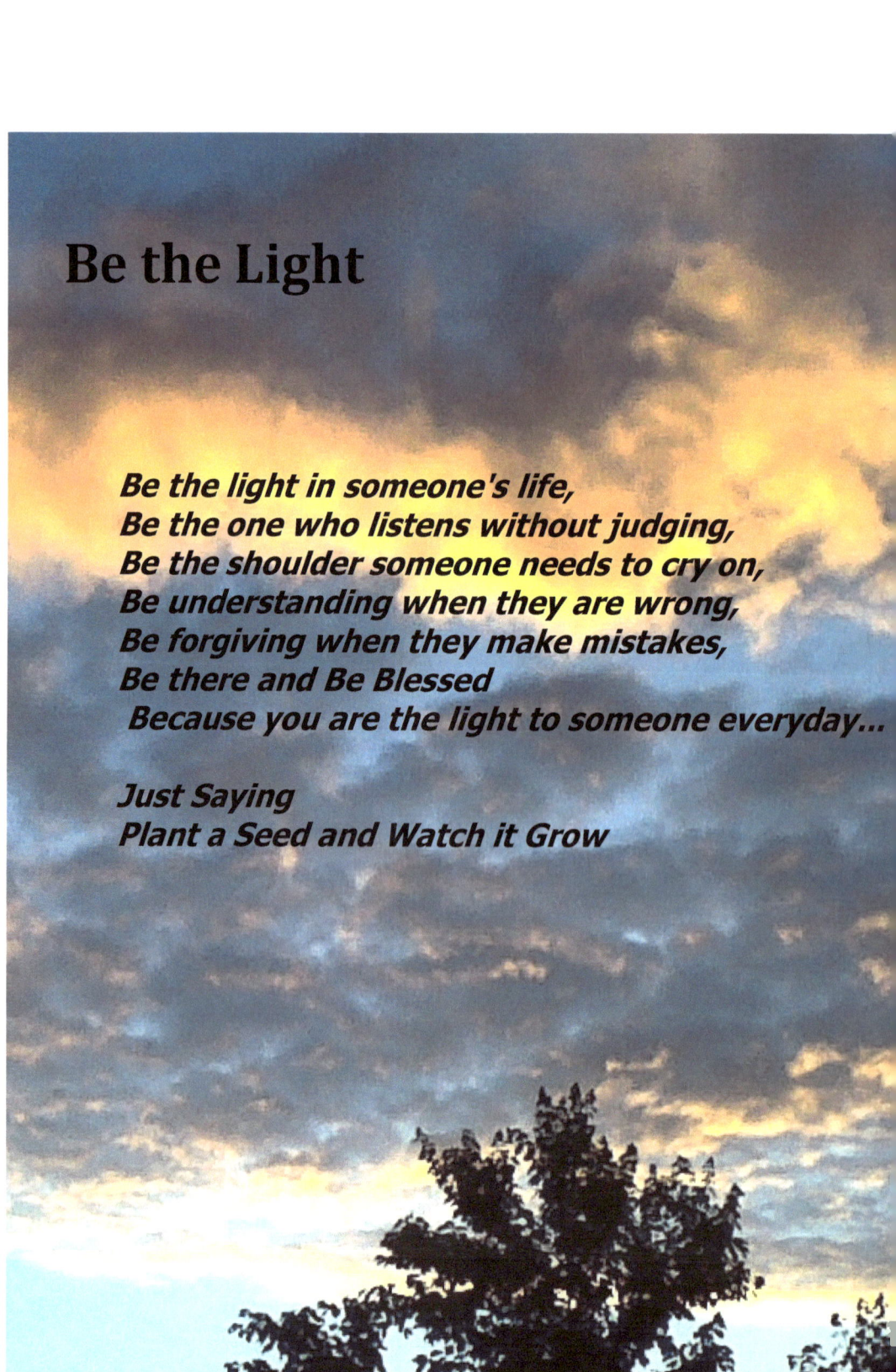

Be the Light

Be the light in someone's life,
Be the one who listens without judging,
Be the shoulder someone needs to cry on,
Be understanding when they are wrong,
Be forgiving when they make mistakes,
Be there and Be Blessed
 Because you are the light to someone everyday...

Just Saying
Plant a Seed and Watch it Grow

Lonely

I Hunger to Feel Your Touch

The Tears I Bleed

Hurt me so Much

I Journey Alone in a World

No One to Hold Me,

No Special Girl

Now I Feel so Lonely,

In this place I call home,

Having No one to call my Own

I Crave You to Hold Me so Tenderly

As I Journey

This World Lost and Lonely

Waiting to Feel your Loving Touch

Showing me, Girl

You Love Me all so Much

But yet,

I still Sit Here Brokenhearted

Knowing our love can Never be Started

Be Who we Are

A single guy that wants to be married, says
'I will do everything I can to make it work '
A married guy that wants to be single, says
'I did everything I could'

If we stop being who we want to be
and just be who we are,
This would be the first step to knowing
who we ready can be. . .

Just saying,
Plant a Seed and Watch it Grow

Oneness...

The *Desire* to belong is one of our most Basic Needs
This is because being *Alone* is too Hard for Us to *Bear*...

When we are *Alone* we *Experience* a sense of *Oneness*
But we feel the need to Fit in Somewhere or with *Someone*...
Then we Feel Safe but not always *Happy*

To Discover who you really *Are*
 You need to Understand Oneness
Before you can Truly Share Yourself

Be Blessed

Walk in Peace and Be Blessed for Who you are

Hold your love ones tight

Because soon they will fly away

God and Love are found

Only in a True Heart

Let it beat Long , Strong and Loud

      Just Saying

Plant and Seed and Watch it Grow

The Teacher

What's the only thing that will always tell the Truth.....?

Time . . .

Because Time will show Truth ...

I Do not Stand on a Pedestal,

For this is for Preaching . . .

I Teach without Speaking a Word,

So my Work is Never Heard...

We must remember

The more one Speaks,

The less one listen...

Benefit comes from What is There,

Usefulness comes from What is not There...

To build four wall and a roof

You beneficial from what it there

But it's the emptiness made for the doors and windows

That made the house useful

It's ok to make Mistakes,

It's the Wise man that Learns from Them. . .

But time is what Teaches us,

Not do it Again...

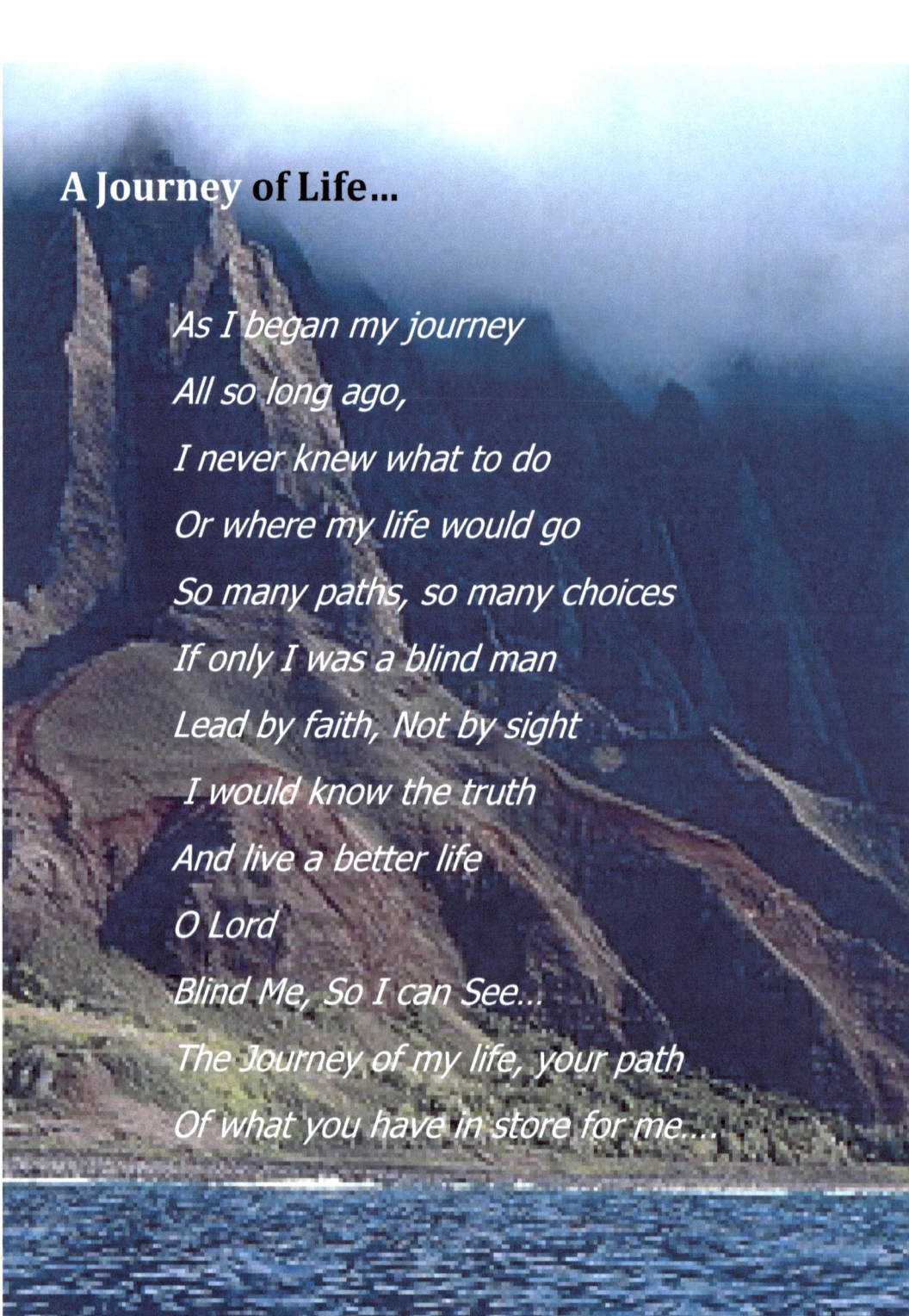

A Journey of Life...

As I began my journey

All so long ago,

I never knew what to do

Or where my life would go

So many paths, so many choices

If only I was a blind man

Lead by faith, Not by sight

I would know the truth

And live a better life

O Lord

Blind Me, So I can See...

The Journey of my life, your path

Of what you have in store for me....

I AM WHO I AM...

As time moves on I reflect

Nothing I did I Regret

Some things I did Right

Many I did wrong

But all these things made me Strong

If I could change a few

But then??? Who knew???

Those things made me the Man I Am...

If I Changed them I wouldn't

Be the dad I Am

A Grandfather to little Cam (Cameron)

A Love lost

A Soulmate not Founded

I'll be DAMN

I AM WHO I AM

A MAN, A BROTHER

A SON, A FATHER

A FRIEND, A LOVER

A SAGE

A POET like no other...

And YOU Know....

I AM WHO I AM

Beautiful Words

Beautiful words are nice
But to say them without showing the love or doing the action
Means Nothing
Like a flower that bears no fruit
Nice to see but you can't feel the joy inside...

Just saying
Plant a Seed and Watch it Grow...

You can't take it with you

For sure there a few things on Earth you can't take with you

Your **Heart**, Your **Body** and Your **Mind**

But you can leave behind

Your **Love**, Your **Essence** and Your **Memories**

So share your life with someone

So you can live forever in their **Heart**, their **Mind** and their **Life**...

Just saying

Plant a seed and watch it grow

Be Heard

We never have to hold our feelings inside
Whether we express ourselves
Through speech, poetry or photography
Everyone of us has a voice with something to say,
Now go out and be heard....

Just saying
Plant a Seed and Watch it Grow

Now Risen...

Only speaking, does not teach anything
If you are to teach and learn
One must also listen ....
To be Risen

Just saying,
So Plant a Seed and Watch it Grow...

www.ingramcontent.com/pod-product-compliance
Lightning Source LLC
Chambersburg PA
CBHW041627220426
43663CB00001B/33